"In *The Simple Book of Infinity*, ĐƠN GIẢN takes century-old concepts and distills them into bite-size wisdom you can embody in this moment. It's one of those books that will read differently every time you pick it up. Sit back, relax and enjoy the ride of your being with this little companion by your side." ~ *Amir Karkouti, American author of What the F**k Are the Three Principles? and Lessons From My Coach*

"ĐƠN GIẢN's words pry open the infinite and hand me the paradox of belonging -- to one another, to ourselves, to the universe. We are all unique and we are never alone. Shall we dance?" ~ *Robert C. Koehler, American syndicated newspaper columnist, peace journalist, and author of Courage Grows Strong at the Wound*

"This book interrupts your thinking and entices you to WONDER beyond what you already know." ~ *Dominic Scaffidi, Toronto, Canada, Master Certified Coach (ICF) and 3 Principles Practitioner*

"*The Simple Book of Infinity* is indeed that. It is…simple. But whilst we might never be able to totally understand infinity, we can acquire enough knowledge in a lifetime to elucidate us in knowing that being 'simple' is truly to be enriched. Something which Leonardo da Vinci named: 'the ultimate sophistication' and Coco Chanel called: 'The keynote of all true elegance.' But what is *The Simple Book of Infinity* about? For me personally in *The Simple Book Of Infinity* I got to recognise and indeed notice ĐƠN GIẢN's 'hidden' revelations, in that some of the GREATEST things in life are so beautifully simple we often take them for granted." ~ *Bob Burns, Scottish hypnotherapist and spiritual healer*

Dedication

*The following understandings emerged over countless
experiences surrendering to being laughed,
though you need not laugh to see
what's there to be seen.*

This is about and for ALL of you.

Love,
ĐƠN GIẢN

How it started   How it's going

Infinity is a big topic.

The biggest!

It can't get any bigger than that…or can it?

By its nature, or definition, infinity is constantly expanding.

Take all the time you need with that statement
or any other in *The Simple Book of Infinity*.

Savor the words and gently digest them.

Read this for the feel of it, like trying on new pants
that look great and you're hoping they will fit.

Your infinite imagination supply is always available.

No matter how big you imagine it is, your infinite imagination supply is bigger than that - and it's always on.

Same for your infinite creativity and spontaneity supplies.

Your infinite perception supply is always available.

Perception is spontaneously created by
the meanings you imagine in each new NOW.

Your infinite perspective supply is always available.

Sometimes we perceive clearly, and sometimes we don't.

This back and forth rhythm of life is between understanding, and temporary, innocent misunderstandings.

The difference can be felt, though we don't always notice.

There is always more to notice, and you can never notice it all.

But! - your infinite noticing supply is always available.

You can calibrate your powers of observation to notice the extraordinary in the ordinary and the unfamiliar in the familiar.

Just noticing this way reveals ripple effects,
or *implications;* evidence of prior learning.

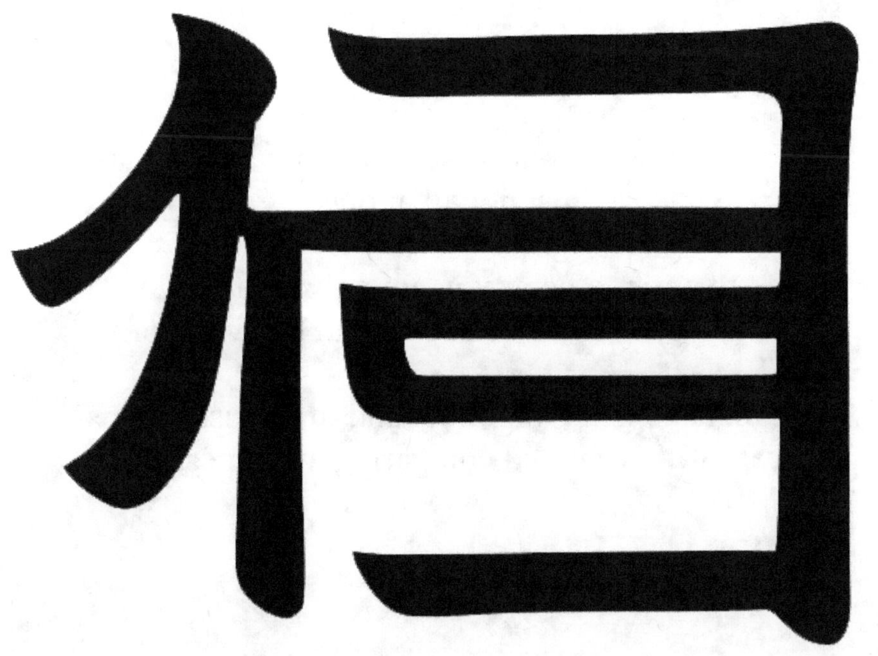

Your infinite awareness supply is always available,
just not all at once.

In any moment, you are only aware of a
tiny fraction of what exists to be aware of.

Language is an imperfect and imprecise means
of sharing and comparing awareness.

Your infinite word supply is always available.

Neither words nor experiences have inherent meaning.

Your meaning-making mechanism is your thinking.

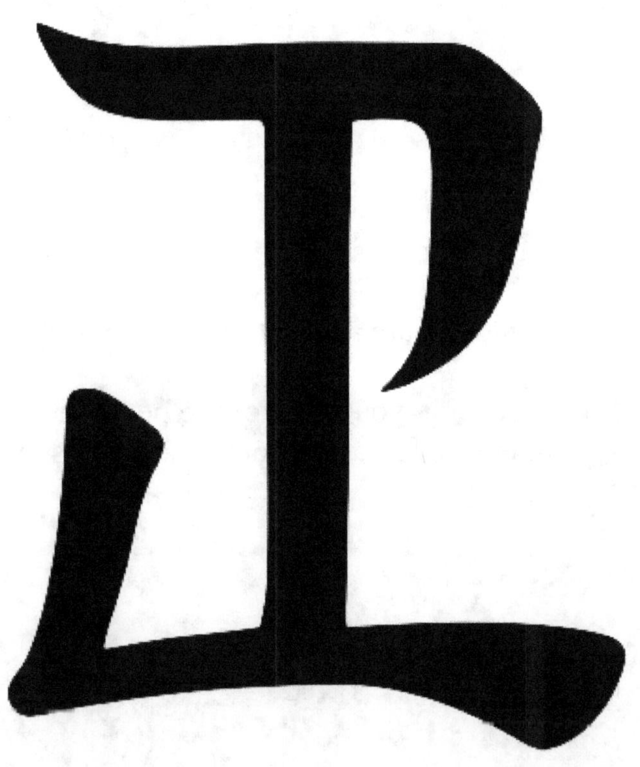

The Nature of Thought exists *before thinking* and *beyond words*.

Words only point, and are not that which is being pointed to.

The meaning you make of the perception
you spontaneously create is your unique perspective.

The infinite formless energy of the Universe is one spiritual being expressing itself in infinite forms (human and otherwise).

That makes self awareness and individuality
the original paradox.

Such apparent contradictions are not puzzles or riddles to solve, but rather the beauty of nature to notice and appreciate.

Ubuntu is often translated as: I am because *we are*.

We are all part of that infinite formless oneness,
only sometimes thinking our form is separate or alone.

This is a common example of
a temporary, innocent misunderstanding.

Your infinite Thought supply is always available.

It's like a Universal radio transmitter is
always broadcasting simultaneously on all frequencies.

You can only ever tune in to a tiny fraction
of the infinite Thought supply.

Thoughts you treat as true, even without awareness,
become your personal thinking.

In real-time, personal thinking spontaneously creates
meanings and perceptions we call feelings or emotions.

Sometimes we innocently misunderstand this,
not perceiving it clearly.

Your infinite storytelling supply is always available.

What seems possible and not possible
depends only on the storyteller's perspective.

Your infinite possibility supply is always available.

Anything is possible!

The first unit of a ruler can be infinitely subdivided.

The same again between unit markers 1 and 2.

Is the infinity between 0 and 2
bigger than the single unit infinities?

Your infinite paradox supply is always available.

Infinitely big and infinitely small are the same.

The more you understand, the less you know.

Your infinite curiosity supply is always available.

Not knowing is yessing curiosity.

Instead of concentrate and focus,
relax and notice.

May the allow be with you.

Your infinite mystery supply is always available.

Wondering "why?" evokes your infinite storytelling supply.

Thoughts are inevitable; believing them is optional.

倚

Your infinite synchronicity supply is always available.

The ubiquity of synchronicities is obscured
by temporary, innocent misunderstandings.

Your infinite misunderstanding supply is always available.

A wave is never separate from the ocean.

You are never separate from
the infinite formless energy of the Universe.

We are eternal.

Your infinite life supply is always available.

Your infinite simplicity supply is always available.

Infinite complexity too.

Simplicity is only as complicated as you make it.

You can always simplify.

You have the right to remain simple - and infinite!

Your infinite infinity supplies are always available.

Your infinite laughter supply is always available.

Laughter is breath plus sound, same as speaking,
but without words or thinking.

You can explore laughter like a fun and noisy meditation,
independent of funny or any other conditions.

Laughter is an all access pass to the entire Universe,
when you surrender to being laughed.

If it is true about laughter, it is true about life.

Laughter is a fractal of life.

Laughter is the stem cell of personal development.

Laughter is the sound of harmony of all spiritual teachings.

You can both lose yourself
and find yourself in laughter.

Laughter shines your inner light
on gifts you've always had but don't always see.

You are perfect in ways you will never know.

Laughter does not clear the mind,
it helps you notice the mind clears itself.

Your mental immune system works flawlessly:
new understandings simply replace old misunderstandings.

Your infinite wellbeing supply is always available.

You can always choose to laugh.

Every breath is an opportunity to laugh.

Laughter is the sound of joyful breathing.

To learn about cells,
look through a microscope.

To learn about stars,
look through a telescope.

To learn about yourself,
look through your laugh.

About the images

Except for the two author photos and two memes with words at the beginning and end of the book, all the images in *The Simple Book of Infinity* were created using the following AI prompt:

> Use simple, minimalist, black/white Main Chinese Hieroglyph style, without depicting actual words in Chinese or any other language, to create a single character image suitable as a philosophy book illustration accompanying the following words:

This prompt was repeated for the words from each page of text. Google Translate, as well as humans fluent in Chinese, Japanese, and Korean confirmed none of the images contain recognized words with commonly understood meanings in those languages.

The intention was to create Chinese gibberish so the reader can notice any meanings attributed to these images are being created by the reader's infinite imagination and perception supplies.

Most of the AI images were generated using Freepik, with a few from PIXLR, and one each from DALL-E and Kapwing.

Thanks to Shashiprabha Jinathissa for prepping the image files for publication.

Discussion Guide

1. Pick any sentence or page. Exchange infinite perspective supplies with one or more other people.

2. Select any one of the infinite supplies mentioned in this book. What can you notice about it in your experience?

3. What infinite supplies not mentioned in this book can you discover in your experience?

4. What *implications* of discovering these infinite supplies can you already begin to imagine or notice NOW?

5. What innocent misunderstandings did this book reveal in your experience? What happened when you noticed them?

6. Describe your infinite storytelling supply on your easiest and most difficult days.

7. Give an example of a choice you stopped making and turned into a rule you don't actually have to follow.

8. How can you put others first without putting yourself second?

9. What question does your infinite curiosity supply want to explore next?

10. Look around until you notice some part of your infinite opportunity supply. Take spontaneously inspired action!

11. Give personal examples showing "progress is the result that occurs when we stop making trouble for ourselves."

12. Your infinite worthiness supply is always available. Knowing that, what will you no longer settle for?

13. Allow your infinite laughter supply to flow for 15 seconds, then one minute, then five minutes. What do you notice?

14. Compare your impressions of the images in this book before and after learning they were designed as Chinese gibberish.

15. What are some ways you can help someone understand something you found useful from this book?

Ways to continue the conversation

- Join the Infinity Laughter group.

- Book ĐƠN GIẢN as a podcast guest or for an event.

- Start a book club, or read/discuss the book in an existing club.

Acknowledgements

Thanks to all the past and current members of Infinity Laughter, formerly called Laughter Gym, with special appreciation for: Amanda Caldwell, Bachan Singh, Bianca Spears, Devon Webster, Isabelle Verez, Janette Leibhardt, Jean Wilkerson, Martin Wiech, Sharon Law (RIP), and Tina Ziegler.

Thanks to my fellow volunteer coaches in the Heartfelt Presence community, and all the guests who join us to listen for a good feeling.

Thanks to Alan D. Thompson, Amy Hardison, Eric Lofholm, Harry ACL, Liz Forrest, Steve Hardison, Tanya Alvarez, and the rest of The Ultimate Coach Facebook group.

Thanks to Dominic Scaffidi, Richard Gordon Kelly, and Tibi Sátor for coaching and space to nurture ideas.

Thanks to David Migliore, Jason Brozek, Jonathan Daddis, Paul Lehto, Ryan Simbai Jenkins, and Scott Phillips for friendship and deep dive conversations.

Thanks to Carly Pearl, Jamie Smart, and Rob Brezsny for inspiration.

Thanks to my father, Joel Berman, for seemingly believing in me even when not understanding me.

About the author

ĐƠN GIẢN is the Vietnamese word for SIMPLE. In Saigon, many young Vietnamese adults study English and adopt English names. This inspired American life coach Dave Berman to adopt ĐƠN GIẢN as his Vietnamese 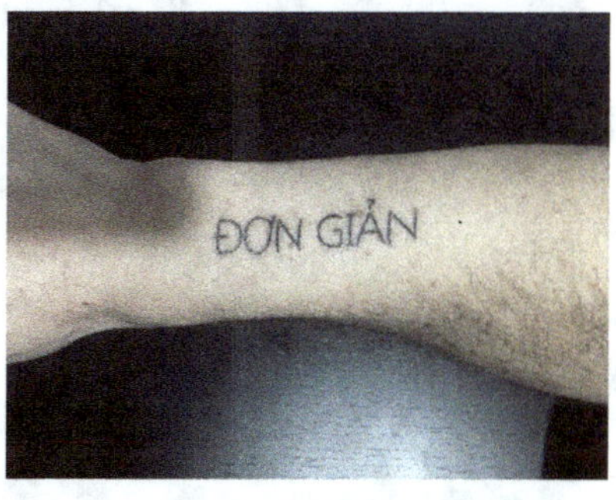
name in July 2023. He says he knows how to be Dave; he is learning to be SIMPLE.

Seeds of the ideas in *The Simple Book of Infinity* were planted during Dave's first stay in Saigon, from 2017-2019. He was on an indefinite international laughter adventure called the Help World Laugh Tour, and vowed to browse the planet for a new place to call home. Saigon became Home Chi Minh City.

When Covid started, Dave was visiting Melbourne, Australia. He only intended to stay 30 days, but that became three years. While in Oz, hosting daily online Laughter Gym sessions fertilized and nurtured the seeds of this book.

In February 2023, Dave returned to Vietnam. His game plan: fuck around and find out! Experiment. Play. Discover what is new and different, about both the city and his way of being.

The first stop on arrival was 23/9 Park. It felt like the completion of a pilgrimage, returning to the special place of hundreds of public laughter sessions years earlier. To Dave's delight, he was greeted there by peace lilies (see photo).

Amidst the many adjustments to Saigon life, Laughter Gym remained constant - more so for the participants around the world than for Dave. Starting at 9:30am Melbourne time meant 5:30am in Saigon.

The daily experiences surrendering to being laughed continued germinating the seeds blossoming on these pages. Then the fucking around suddenly led to a lot of finding out!

All on one day, Dave moved to the Thảo Điền area of Saigon, renamed Laughter Gym to Infinity Laughter, bumped the start time to 8am, and added the ĐƠN GIẢN tattoo.

In these still early days of Dave's journey learning to be ĐƠN GIẢN, several old habits have already fallen away and new ways of thinking and communicating have emerged.

This is not a short term transition and will never be complete. *The Simple Book of Infinity* joins Dave's previous books, videos, audios, trainings, and coaching programs, each like a cairn marking the path of his personal evolution.

The environment supporting this perpetual growth is Dave's infinite imagination supply and the *imagination partnerships* he creates to support other people becoming who they want to be.

For more information, please visit

https://DaveBermanCoaching.com

DaveBermanCoaching.com/join

www.ingramcontent.com/pod-product-compliance
Lightning Source LLC
Chambersburg PA
CBHW071053260726
48661CB00006B/2251